LIFT YOUR EYES UP TO JESUS

By

JANET DOLAK

LIFT YOUR EYES UP TO JESUS

A book of poems inspired by God

Written by Janet Dolak

Illustrated by Jesse Stryker

ISBN # 9780997931013

TABLE OF CONTENTS

LIFT YOUR EYES UP TO JESUS

Lift your eyes up to Jesus.
Give to Him all of your praise.
Lifting your eyes upon Jesus.
Loving Him all of your days.

Lift your eyes up to Jesus.
He will keep watch over you.
Lifting your eyes upon Jesus.
Know that He's loving you too.

Lift your voice up to Jesus.
Tell Him your story so true.
Lifting your voice up to Jesus.
Knowing your life will be new.

Lift your arms up to Jesus.
He holds you close to His heart.
Lifting your arms up to Jesus.
His love will never depart.

WHERE DID I SEE YOU TODAY?

Where did I see You today?
In the face of an innocent child.
Where else did I see You today?
In the calming of those who were riled.

Where were You working today?
In the wind and the clouds and the rain.
Where else were You working today?
In the hearts of those filled with pain.

What were You doing today?
Comforting those who were sad.
What else were You doing today?
Giving Grace to those who'd been bad.

Who were You helping today?
All who believe in My Son.
Who else were You helping today?
Any who know He's the One.

But what about those who don't know?
For them to believe you must pray.
And the ones who refuse to believe?
You must show them that He is the way.

Where did I see You today?
In the colorful trees all around.
Where else did I see You today?
In My love for mankind that abounds.

Where will I see You tomorrow?
Just open your eyes and you'll see.
In everything you see tomorrow,
Just look and there I will be.

5

I LAY MY HEAD UPON A ROCK

I lay my head upon a rock;
The dreams that come – they will not stop.
Like Jacob with his ladder glowing.
Angels coming – angels going.

My mind at rest – it will not be
Its constant thoughts on Thee, on Thee,
How glorious these thought abounding
Come to me in love resounding.

I lay my head upon Thy knee
My eyes You open ere to see.
Heaven's treasures piling up.
Your love overflows our every cup.

While thoughts may wander here and there.
Sometimes they go without a care.
Always to return to You dear Jesus.
Always Grace and love You give us.

I bow my head and give my heart.
My thoughts from You no longer dart.
I'll climb the ladder to the top.
My love for You will never stop.

TRUST

We must trust You
When we don't know what to do.
We must trust You
Because You'll always see us through
We must trust You

We must trust You
When darkness overcomes us.
We must trust You
Because Your light will guide our way.
We must trust You

We must trust You
When the road ahead is blocked.
We must trust you
Because the door You will unlock.
We must trust You

We must trust You
When we sure are overwhelmed.
We must trust You
Because You're surely at the helm.
We must trust You

We must trust You
When we're hurt and do not care.
We must trust You
And know You always will be there.
We must trust You

We must trust You
We must let you in our hearts
We must trust You
Because You never will depart.
We must trust You

We must trust You
Trust You'll hold us in Your arms.
We must trust You
And know You'll keep us from all harm.
We must trust You

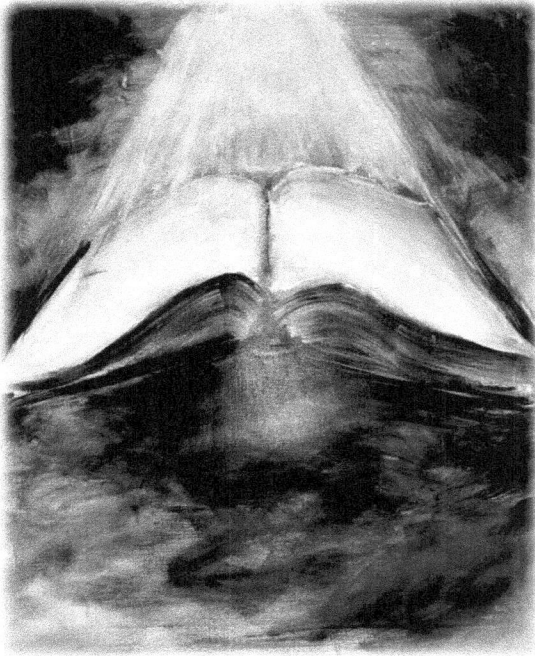

RESISTANCE FROM ABOVE

When the salesman tries to sell you
All the extras for your car,
You hold your ground resisting –
Money only goes so far.

He pushes and entices with
All the things that you might like.
From sunroof, cruise and stereo
To a rack that holds your bike.

The more he says, "You need this."
And the more he says, "Why not?"
The harder to resist it all.
Gee, it's really not a lot.

So You say, "Just this one thing I'll get.
Well, maybe that one too."
And soon instead of simply base,
Your whole bankroll you blew.

It's the same when you are dealing
With the devil and his kin.
Resisting isn't easy cuz
He really wants to win.

He says, "Just once. It's simple.
It won't hurt you this one time."
And if your feet aren't grounded
Then his next line is, "You're MINE!"

You know you're only human.
And as human you will sin.
And if you don't love Jesus,
Then your future will look grim.

Temptations will surround you.
You can't control that part.
But if you give in to them,
They'll eat away your heart.

The only thing that matters
Is the knowledge of God's love.
And how He sent His Son to us;
Resistance from above.

You know what's right and what is wrong.
You know what you should do.
Pray that Jesus holds your hand.
Pray that He'll see you through.

For if the Lord is by your side
The devil can't get in.
You're saved from death eternally.
He rescues you from sin.

THE STAIN

A stain is on your shirt
So a sweater you must wear
To cover up the carelessness
So no one knows it's there.

But when you break God's law,
And a stain is on your heart,
A sweater's not the answer.
Not even a small start.

For God can see your actions;
All things you think and do.
To try to cover up your sins
Will never get you through.

You have to ask forgiveness;
You must believe in Christ.
You know the crucifixion;
To be humbled in His sight.

That is the only way, you see
To cover up that stain.
The blood of Jesus Christ, our Lord
Will cleanse just like the rain.

He died to save us from our sins.
He died to set us free.
He rose again – God's miracle
And that saved you and me.

So if you think a sweater
Is the answer to your fall,
Remember of God's sacrifice
Christ died to save us all.

CONTROL WE RELEASE

We say our prayers,
We ask Your presence,
Then we feel Your peace.
We know You listen
To all we ask
Your grace is in our reach.

You touch our lives
In every way.
Sometimes we do not know
That what we do
Is a prompt from You.
We learn this and we grow.

When things go right
We might forget
Who to give credit to.
But if we stop
And look around
We know to credit You.

When minds are closed
To new ideas
Control we must release.
Please help us see
That things won't work
Unless it's You we please.

DO YOU SEE?

Do You see what we are seeing?
Will You tell us what it means?
Will You speak to our salvation?
Is that what the voices scream?

Are You soon to be among us?
Will You let us see Your face?
Are we lifted up beside You?
Are we prepared to leave this place?

We want to know You, Jesus.
We want to worship You.
Do You see what we are seeing?
Will You tell us that it's true?

Every voice we hear that tells us,
That You're coming back to stay.
We want to be near Jesus.
We look forward to that day.

14
CREATION

Now is the time to tell the story
Of how everything came to be.
Of how the earth became so big,
Of how God made the sea.

The atmosphere was needed for air
So the sky and the land were made two.
He said, "Now let's see. There's more that I need.
To stop here never would do."

So He put in the sky a ball of fire
And called it a sun shining bright.
And nighttime was made on the other side
With the moon making everything right.

Then the land He dried up and scattered about
The oceans were filled to the rim.
But He didn't stop there; He wasn't quite done.
Without more things all would be grim.

The land was filled with grains and fruits
And different mammals galore.
All kinds of fish, and turtles and whales
He put on the ocean's floor.

He made birds on wings and other things.
He made mountains and beautiful trees.
He made gardens on earth and stars in the sky
But had nothing to fall on their knees.

So He took some mud and made a form.
It was quite a sight to behold.
He called it man and gave him a chore;
To rule over all he was told.

But man needed help. It was lonesome for him
So God put the man down to sleep.
He took out a rib and made man a wife.
And promised them safe He would keep.

He looked all around and saw all was good.
The earth was created at last.
So He sat on His throne being happy and tired.
This happened long ago in the past.

YOU'RE UNDER MY UMBRELLA

When the rain falls down around us
Don't worry you'll get wet;
Because I'm here beside you
And you'll never need to fret.

For you're under my umbrella.
I'll protect you from the rain.
You're under my umbrella
And I'll walk you down the lane.

Whenever you feel threatened,
When danger comes to roost,
Remember that I'm with you
If you ever need a boost.

For you're under my umbrella.
I'll protect you from the rain.
You're under my umbrella
And I'll walk you down the lane.

When troubles seem abundant
And things don't go just right,
Ask and I will help you.
I'll see you through the fight.

For you're under my umbrella.
I'll protect you from the rain.
You're under my umbrella
And I'll walk you down the lane.

You'll see dark clouds on occasion
But silver linings are there too.
It helps to know I'm with you.
You know I'll see you through.

For you're under my umbrella.
I'll protect you from the rain.
You're under my umbrella
And I'll walk you down the lane.

WHAT IS IT YOU WANT ME TO DO?

What is it that I should gain from today?
What is it You want me to do?
How is it You want me to walk in Your Way?
What activities should I pursue?

Do You want me to read some more of Your Book?
Do You want me to just sit and pray?
Should I pick out a cloud, then sit back and look?
Should I seek someone out I should sway?

Please speak to me God, in Your special voice.
Please tell me, Your message to hear.
In following you, I don't have a choice
But Your message just has to be clear.

So what do You want me to do today?
I'm listening so that I will know.
This need to be near You just won't go away.
That need for You leaves me aglow.

I'll do what You say, an honor to do.
I'll listen and do it Your way.
Whether it's old or something brand new
Just ask and I'll do it today.

FATHER FORGIVE THEM

Father, forgive them, for they know not what they do.
Father, forgive them, for they don't know to love You.
We'll talk about You daily.
We'll show them how we pray.
Father, forgive us, for we have not taught them true.

Surly, so surly, we'll give You praise each day.
Surly, so surly, we'll try to lead the way.
We'll read the Holy Bible.
We'll sing about Your son.
Surly, so surly, You'll show us what to say..

Surely, yes surely. Your truth they'll come to know.
Surely, yes surely. There'll be no need for woe.
They soon will want to love You.
They'll kneel down at Your feet.
Surely, yes surely. Their love for You will show.

MOTHERS

Everyone has a mother.
This is a well-known fact.
We had to come from somewhere,
So a mother no one lacks.

But what really is a mother?
What makes a mother true?
A mother's more than someone
Who holds a babe who's new.

A mother staves off hunger;
Sometimes giving of her own.
A mother keeps us comfortable;
Her arms can keep us warm.

A mother sacrifices
To be sure we have enough.
She'll kiss away our hurts and pains
When the road we're on gets rough.

Unconditional is a mother's love
No matter what we do.
She overlooks, defends and cries.
Forgives us through and through.

A mother's always watching
To be sure we're on God's path.
She steps in to protect us
So we do not suffer wrath.

A mother watches as we grow.
She guides us on our way.
She prays that God will always be
Beside us day by day.

A mother teaches every day
In many different ways.
A mother's job is more than to
Be sure her child obeys.

Her job is to be nurturing,
Her job is to be there
Whenever she is needed.
A mother's job is care.

And when her child is grown up
Does a mother just forget?
He's grown and now he's on his own.
Not true, that you can bet.

Her job is never ending
It goes on all her life.
There's always someone needing
Her help to deal with strife.

Sometimes the tears she sheds are sad,
Sometimes the tears are glad.
Sometimes the laughter overtakes.
The good defeats the bad.

A mother doesn't have to
Give birth to one who's dear.
A woman can become a mom
When needed by one near.

And who does Mom rely on
To help her with this task?
Why, God's the one she turns to
And He answers when she asks.

22

WHAT IF NOBODY COMES?

What if we call out
And nobody comes?
What if we ask
And nobody cares?

How can we tell them
If nobody shows up?
How will they know?
They'll be unaware!!

We want to share
What we know about Jesus.
We want to tell
The world what we know.

But first we must have
Some people to listen.
How can we tell them
If nobody shows?

The table is set.
The people are ready.
We're eager to share
The love that You give.

The books are all laid out.
The nametags are plenty.
We're all here and ready
To tell how You lived.

But not just Your life
Will we tell to the listeners.
We'll tell of Your death;
How You did die for us.

And how we'll be with You
Throughout life eternal.
These are some things
We'd like to discuss.

But how can we do it
If no one will listen.
Nobody came,
So we cannot share.

The hallways are quiet
The chairs will stay empty.
Nobody came so
They'll stay unaware.

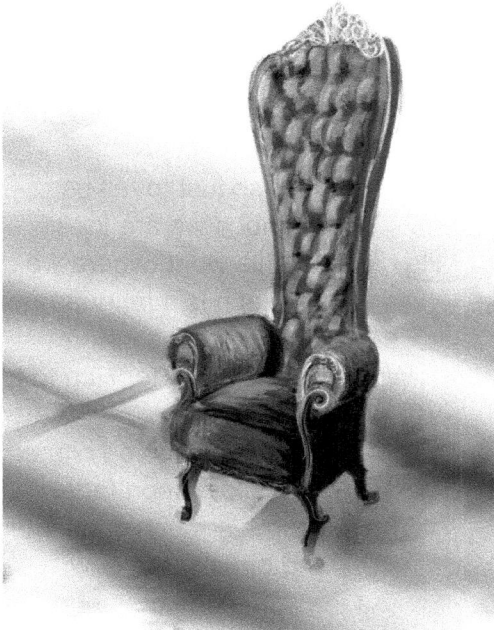

NEW DAYS

As I move down the road
With the sun at my back
The red glow soon covers the land.
The trees are all pretty
With leaves of all shades
Shinning bright when the sun shows so grand.

And on the horizon
The mountaintops shine
With low flying clouds overhead.
This new day begins
With all kinds of promise
Which glows in the trees gold and red.

For God speaks so clearly
If only we listen.
He tells us He's there by our side.
The land in its beauty
Is part of His language.
He gives it. We take it in stride.

And so just to tell us
How much we are loved.
He gives us this world where we dwell.
His speech is a language.
We know it as nature
What more is there for Him to tell?

As the sun climbs up higher
The colors soon fade.
The sky turns a much subtler blue.
The birds settle down
As the sun shine gets brighter.
Each day is so wonderfully new.

25
The water that flows
Down the river below.
It glistens as rays touch each drop.
This day is awakening
With, oh, so much beauty.
Our hurrying we want to stop.

A mysterious mist
Is off to the East
Where the warm air takes over the cold.
There's no two alike.
Each day is made new
For God doesn't use any molds.

It must be the same
For me and for you.
We're different as any can see
And God loves each one
Of us just as we are.
He made us; that's how it should be.

26
PALM BRANCHES WAVING

Palm branches waving
Triumphant He comes.
Everyone's cheering;
Announcing the Son.

He came to save us.
Our king comes today
Into the city
Where crowds line the way.

The colt proudly carries
Our Savior on high
Into the city
Where He's going to die.

But now He's triumphant
As slowly He rides.
Everyone's cheering
As Jesus arrives!

27

MY PRAYER IS THIS

Please Dear God, Most gracious and loving God. You are wonderful and glorious.

I thank You for all You do for me and I thank You for loving all of us.

Dear God – I pray, keep us safe today. Bless all of my family too. And then there are my friends; both near and far. I love that You care for them too.

Please Dear Lord, protect all of those who serve to protect and defend us. There are policemen and firemen here at home and there are military both home and away.

Wrap your loving arms around all of them and keep them safe from harm. Comfort those who have lost loved ones and those who have been hurt. Be with them both night and day.

And help me dear God to know what You want and to do what You want me to do. And to follow Your lead and to show it to others.

Help those who are ill or simply don't feel well whether physically or emotionally depressed. Be with those who are traveling and those who serve You. Help them to honor and spread Your good Word.

I ask all of this because You have promised to give us all that we need. Your promise was Jesus and I ask this in His name - and I thank You for caring for me.

AMEN